A bad start

It's a bad start to the morning.
Dad burns the toast. He scowls.

I spill milk on my best top
with an owl on it. I frown.

Mum stands on Pam's tail
and Pam growls.

Then Sid gets a
fright and yowls.

Sam drops a mug on his foot. He howls.

7

In town, we see a big
crowd on the street.

We see a street artist.
She is painting a farmyard
on the bricks.

She adds in brown cows
and ducks and green trees.

We have lunch next.
We tuck into dumplings
with chopsticks.

A clown is juggling three hats.

Now he is juggling tennis rackets. He bows to the crowd.

There is so much to see.

Now we all feel good.

Words to blend

start	morning	foot
toast	fright	hurt
turn	street	artist
painting	farmyard	cool
green	with	lunch
three	much	feel

Before reading

Synopsis: All sorts of things go wrong in the morning so the family decides to go to town. They have fun and go home feeling good after their bad start.

Review phoneme/s: ar or ur

New phoneme: ow

Story discussion: Look at the cover, and read the title together. Ask: *How is Nat feeling? What do you think has happened? Have you ever felt like Nat, when your day has got off to a bad start?* Share children's experiences of this.

Link to prior learning: Display the digraph ow. Remind children that digraphs are two letters that make one sound together. Can they read the digraph ow and say the sound? Display the words *frown, town, owl, crowd*. Encourage children to sound out and blend the words.

Vocabulary check: Yowl – screech. Ask children to read Sid's speech bubble on page 5 with a yowling sound. How do they think Sid is feeling?

Decoding practice: Give children a card with the digraph ow, and cards or magnetic letters for h, l, n, b, t. How many real words can they make and read? (e.g. ow, how, howl, now, bow, town, owl)

Tricky word practice: Display the word *my*. Ask children to circle the tricky bit in the word (the grapheme y, which makes the sound /igh/). Do children know any other tricky words where y makes this sound? (e.g. by) Encourage them to look out for these words in their reading.

After reading

Apply learning: Discuss the story. Can children explain how the family's mood changed from the beginning to the end of the story? Relate this to children's own experience of times when they felt bad to start with, but their mood improved as time went on.

Comprehension

- What idea did Dad have to make everyone feel better?
- Can you remember three fun things the family did in town?
- How did Dan feel at the end? Find a speech bubble that shows this.

Fluency

- Pick a page that most of the group read quite easily. Ask them to reread it with pace and expression. Model how to do this if necessary.
- Turn to page 7, and ask children to read Dad's speech bubble with appropriate pace, expression and enthusiasm.
- Practise reading the words on page 17.

Tricky words review

oh	one	he
my	go	said
into	we	she
have	do	there
so	all	was